KALEIDOSCOPE

COMPUTERS

by
Darcy Lockman

BENCHMARK BOOKS

MARSHALL CAVENDISH
NEW YORK

Series Consultant:
Dr. Paul Benjamin
School of Computer Science and Information Systems
Pace University

Benchmark Books
Marshall Cavendish Corporation
99 White Plains Road
Tarrytown, NY 10591-9001

Library of Congress Cataloging-in-Publication Data
Lockman, Darcy, date.
Computers / by Darcy Lockman.
    p. cm. – (Kaleidoscope)
Includes bibliographical references and index.
Summary: Explains the different parts of a computer and how they work.
ISBN: 0-7614-1045-7
1. Computers—Juvenile literature. [1. Computers.] I. Title. II. Kaleidoscope (Tarrytown, NY)
QA76.23   L63   2000
004—dc21   99-057022

Photo research by Candlepants, Inc.
Cover photo © Image Bank
Picture credits: © Image Bank: 5, 6, 8, 10, 13, 14, 17, 18, 22, 25, 26, 28, 32, 34, 37 (left), 37 (right), 38, 41.
© Photo Researchers: 30, 42. Diagram on page 21 by Gysela Pacheco

Printed in Italy

6 5 4 3 2 1

CONTENTS

ABOUT COMPUTERS

Computers are everywhere. They're behind the checkout counter of your local grocery store. They're in the cars your parents and teachers drive. They're in airports and office buildings and banks. A *computer* is a device that can perform complex calculations—like multiplication—with very little help from a person. Computers can also store an amazing amount of information. Computer technology has become so common that almost everybody in America comes across it every day.

This man has created an entire office on his computer before it has been built. Now he is using virtual reality to help him design the inside.

TYPES OF COMPUTERS

Do you use computers to get on the *Internet* or to write reports for school? Those kinds of computers fall into two categories, *PC*, or personal computer, and *Macintosh*. A PC is a computer made to be used by a single person and can be found in many schools, homes, and offices. The original PCs were made by a company called IBM, so many people call personal computers IBMs. PCs that aren't made by IBM are often called IBM-compatibles, because they use the same programs as IBMs to operate.

Personal computers are used for many things. You can even learn how to play the piano.

A Macintosh is a similar sort of computer but made by a company called Apple. It also has its own operation programs, the basic programs needed to run the computer. Macintosh-operating programs do not work in IBM computers. Since these computers were made to work with graphics and artwork, people who do things such as designing books and magazines use them.

People make designs for all kinds of things using Macintosh computers. This woman is using one to design a die cutter form, a kind of mold that is used to make machine parts.

Design: LAY
File name: 7 7089
Active Job = D:\DATASE902H.DAT   395
loading 90401

9

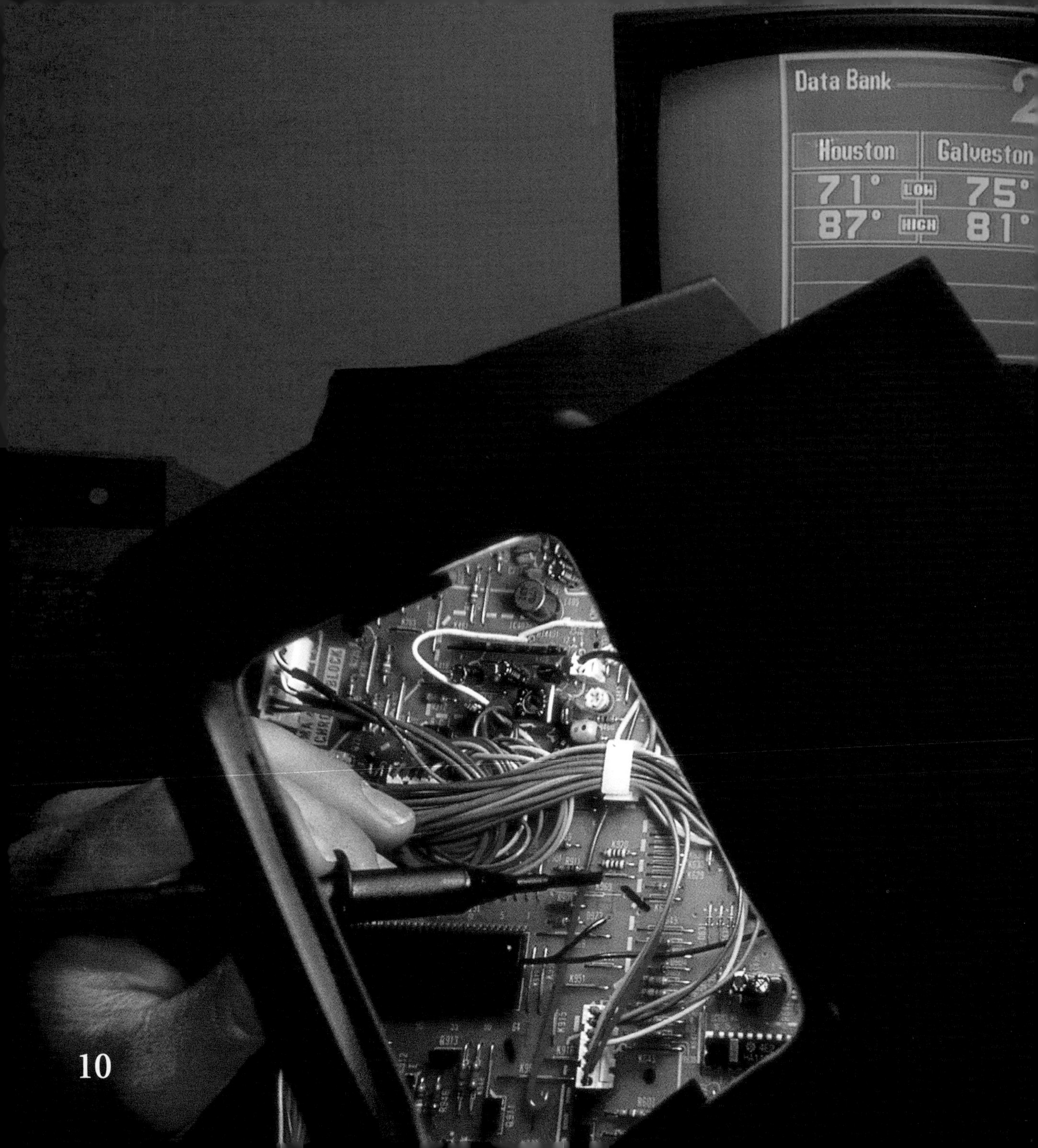
Data Bank
Houston
Galveston
71° LOW 75°
87° HIGH 81°

HOW DOES A
COMPUTER WORK?

Do you know how a car works? A telephone? A television? There are many things we use every day without understanding how they work. Many people use computers without really knowing what's going on inside. But computers are much more interesting —and less intimidating—when we understand how they work.

You probably use a television every day, but have you ever looked inside one or thought about how they work? Like a computer, a television is made of many electronic parts.

A computer has two basic parts—*hardware* and *software*. Hardware is the physical part of a computer. That is, any part you can see or touch, inside or out, like a memory chip, the *keyboard*, or the *computer case*. The computer case is the shell that holds the computer together.

This is a detail of a circuit board, which is inside a computer. The circuit board is a piece of hardware. It helps put what you type on the keyboard onto the screen.

There are four main pieces of hardware that make a computer function. The *memory unit* is one of these. A computer's memory can store huge amounts of information, like an entire phone book or an encyclopedia. Every time you type something and save it on the computer, this is where it is stored. But the memory does more than just hold information.

This tiny computer chip can hold as much information as what's in all your schoolbooks and more.

Some types of memory chips store the instructions that tell the computer how to work. Some instructions are built in the computer. Others, called software, have to be loaded into the memory. Without software, a computer would be like a human body without a brain. The memory unit includes the memory chips and the *hard drive*.

When you learn how to do something new, such as cross-country ski, you keep the memory in a certain part of your brain. When it comes time to ski again, you recall the memory to do it. When you load software into a computer for a game, it is kept in a part of the computer called the memory. When it comes time to play the game, the computer recalls the game software from the memory to play it.

Another of the computer's units is the *input unit*. This is what you use to give the computer instructions. The input unit has two pieces. The first is the *mouse*. A mouse is a handheld device you use to move around the screen. The second is the keyboard.

The keyboard is part of the input unit. Each key you press on the keyboard makes a different electronic signal that it sends to the processing unit.

When you type on the keyboard, each keystroke produces a unique electric signal that is sent to the computer's *processing unit.* The processing unit is the most complex of a computer's units. It contains many very small electronic parts. As the signals pass through the parts, they are translated back into the words, numbers, or symbols you have typed. Then they are sent to a screen or printer—the computer's *output units.* The screen, or monitor, displays what you've typed, or the printer prints it out.

The final piece of hardware is part of many, but not all, computers. It is called a *modem.* A modem is a device that hooks your computer to the Internet.

 Here's how a computer works.

1. Each key you hit or mouse you click sends an electronic signal to the processing unit. 2. The processing unit converts these signals into words, images, or symbols, and sends them to the output units— 3. —the screen, or the printer.

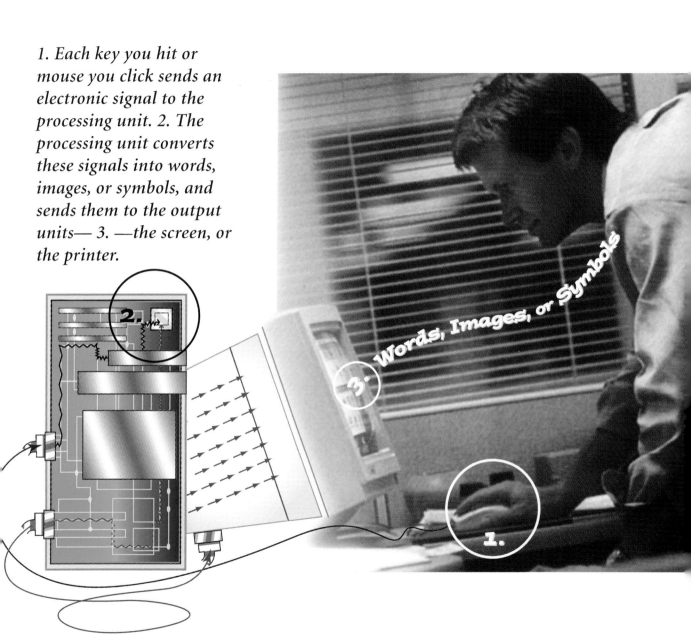

22

Software, mentioned earlier, is a very important part of the computer. Software contains electronic directions that tell the computer how to do very specific things. Think of everything you've done on a computer. Can you name some of those things? You've probably used it to play games, to go online, to write letters. You need software to do all of these. A computer doesn't come with software built-in. It must be loaded into the computer where it is stored in a memory chip or on the hard drive.

A video game is a type of computer called a dedicated computer. *It is designed to do only one thing, in this case run one type of game.*

You can't see software. You can't touch software. What you can see and touch are the packaging software comes in and the disks and CD-ROMs on which the computer instructions are encoded.

Software may come stored on CD-ROM disks like this one. After the disk is put into the slot, the software is read and recorded by the memory.

24

25

Software does not just exist on its own—people called computer programmers write it. They are the people who create the instructions that are on the disk or CD-ROM. They make sure the computer will understand the different types of instructions by writing them in the right computer languages. Computer programmers are responsible for just about everything you can do with your computer.

This computer programmer is writing software that will be used in personal computers.

COMPUTERS PAST AND PRESENT

The modern computer is a wondrous object, but like other technology, it had to evolve to become what it is today. The evolution began in the 1800s when a British mathematician named Charles Babbage designed, but did not build, a machine that could work a lot like a modern computer. In 1930, an American scientist named Vannevar Bush actually built one of the earliest computers, then called a differential analyzer.

An abacus was used to solve math problems by sliding the beads, which stand for numbers, back and forth. It was used in ancient China and other countries and can be thought of as a very early computer.

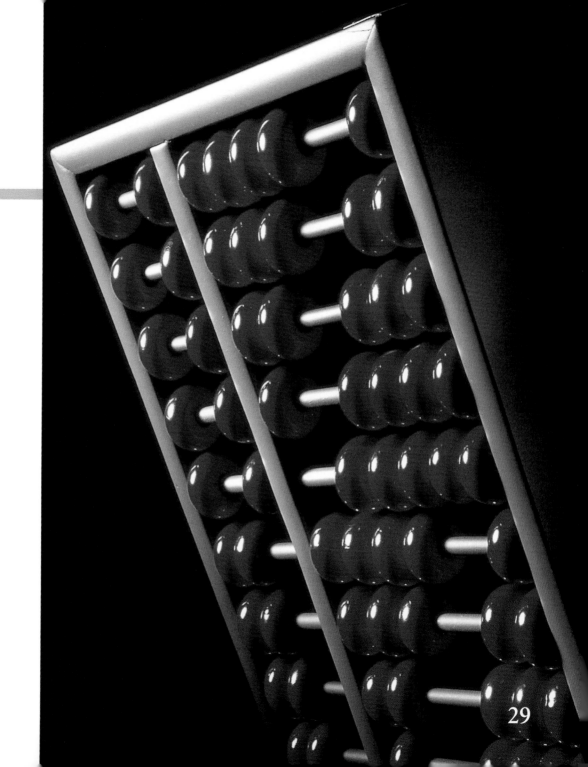

29

Over the next few decades, scientists and engineers worked together to build the first real computers. These first computers were very big, but not very practical. They were were mostly used by the government and universities.

This computer is similar to the first huge computers. It is called a supercomputer and is at use in the NASA/Ames Research Center in California.

Scientists and engineers continued working together to build computers every-day people could use at home or at work. They were finally successful in 1981.

 Because they were so easy to use, the new personal computers became very popular the world over. These children in China are learning all about computers, just like you.

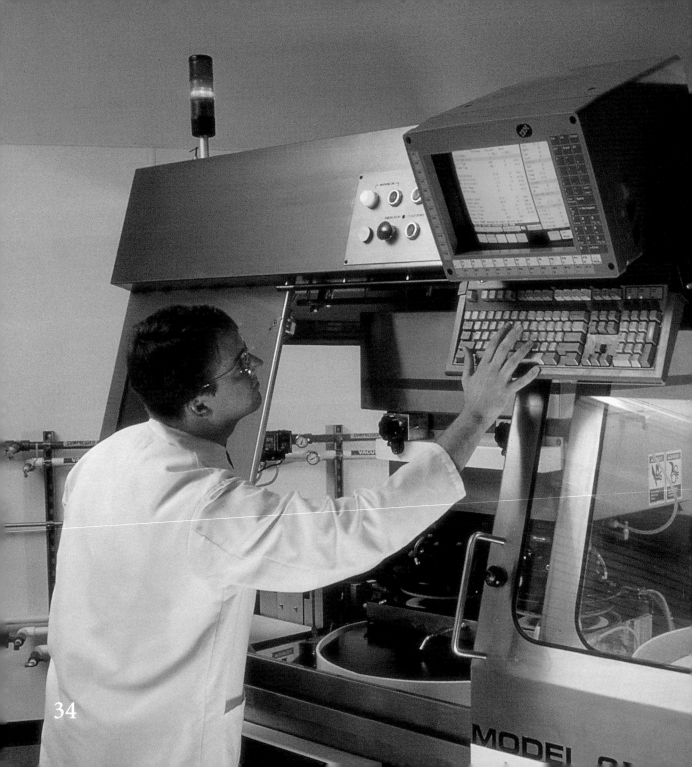

The personal computer was so compact and easy to use that it became very popular. Because so many people wanted to buy computers, computer scientists had all the more reason to keep trying to make computers better. The personal computers got smaller and more powerful. As a result, computers are now very important in our daily lives. And computer scientists are still improving upon computers every day.

Computers will keep getting better as the years go by. Technicians like this one are working to make them faster and more powerful.

WHAT ARE COMPUTERS USED FOR?

Today computers are used in more ways than you could ever count. Libraries use them to check books in and out. Governments use them to store top-secret information. Elevators are run by computer systems. Air traffic controllers rely on them to direct airplanes. Banks use them to keep track of money and accounts.

Computers have changed the way we do many ordinary things. In the past, cashiers typed the prices of items into a cash register and then added them together, along with any tax, by themselves. Now, cashiers just scan price tags. The computer does the rest.

Business people use them to write reports and keep inventory. Writers use computers instead of typewriters to write their books and articles. All of these tasks were around before computers were invented—computers just made them much easier to do. We have become so used to computers, it's hard imagine a world without them.

Computers have changed the way people do business. Today, computers can store and print important documents and send messages with a simple mouse click.

Have you used a computer to connect to the Internet? The Internet is the world's largest computer network, and on it you can find information on just about anything—your favorite band, the latest action movies, the country you need to write a report about. Computers connect to the Internet with modems and phone lines mostly, but also with satellites and cable television wires.

You can find information about almost any subject on the Internet.

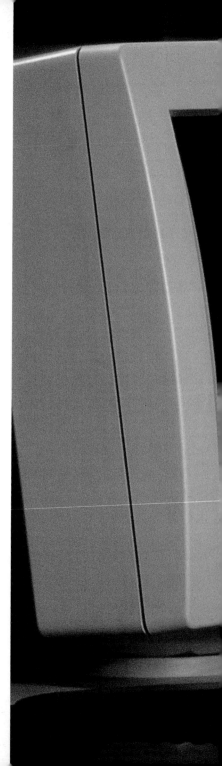

URL: http://www.csu.edu.au/special/...

World Wide Web:
Changing the way we work, learn and play.

The Internet is changing the way people communicate. People all over the world can share information by posting it on websites, or by sending each other e-mails, which arrive much more quickly than regular letters. It has also become a place where people can buy and sell things. No one is really sure how the Internet will change our world, but it will, just as the computer has.

This is an example of a web page. Notice the long rectangular box at the top. If you want to go to a special website this is where you type the address.

GLOSSARY

Computer A machine that can perform a series of complex calculations and in which information and instructions can be stored.

Computer case The body of a computer. It stores a computer's memory unit and electronic parts.

Dedicated computer A computer that can only do one thing. Video games and ATM machines are dedicated computers.

Hard drive The part of a computer's memory that stores the information a user inputs.

Hardware The parts of the computer you can see or touch.

Input unit The computer keyboard and mouse that are used to send electronic signals to the processing unit.

Internet The world's largest computer network; it is a group of computers that share information.

Keyboard The lettered pad that allows a user to type information into a computer.

Macintosh A personal computer made by a company called Apple.

Memory unit   The part of the computer that stores information.

Modem   The piece of hardware that allows a computer to connect to a telephone line.

Monitor   the screen that displays the words and images made by a computer.

Mouse   The handheld device that enables a computer user to move the cursor around the computer screen.

Output unit   The computer's screen and printer.

PC   Stands for personal computer. PCs are computers that use software made for IBM computers.

Processing unit   The part of a computer that reads the electronic signals sent to it by the input unit and does any calculations necessary.

Software   The programs that instruct a computer how to perform various jobs.

FIND OUT MORE

Books:

Billings, Charlene W. *Supercomputers: Shaping the Future.* NY: Facts on File, 1996.

Borman, Jami L. *Computer Dictionary for Kids and Their Parents.* NY: Baron, 1995.

Chambers, Catherine. *Computer.* NH: Heinemann Library, 1998.

Jortberg, Charles A. *Virtual Reality and Beyond.* Kids and Computers Series. MN: Abdo Publishing Company, 1997.

Kazunas, Tomas. *Personal Computers.* True Book series. CT: Children's Press, 1997.

Websites:

History of Computers:
http://www.hitmill.com/computers/computerhx1.html

Study Web: Computers:
http://www.studyweb.com/Computer_Science/

3D Computer Dictionary:
http://207.136.90.76/dictionary/index.html

Kids and Computers:

http://www2.magmacom.com/~dsleeth/

The Ultimate Computer Source:

http://library.advanced.org/25018/

AUTHOR'S BIO

Darcy Lockman is a freelance writer who has written on technology for a number of young adult publications. She lives in New York City.

INDEX

Page numbers for illustrations are in boldface.